The POWER dimension
by Michael Cole

CONTENTS

Intro	2
Spotlight on the Holy Spirit	4
True life experiences	10
Plug in for power	11
Hot or cold?	17
A new person	18
No holding back	24
New horizons	25
That bit more…	31
What next?	32

Cover design: Ross Advertising and Design Limited ·
Designer: Paul Edwards · Inside illustrations: Paulo Baigent ·
Typeset by HWTypesetters, Norwich · Printed by Ebenezer Baylis & Son
Limited, The Trinity Press, Worcester and London ·
© Scripture Union 1994, 130 City Road, London EC1V 2NJ · ISBN 086201 817 X

the power dimension

INTRO

The grandeur of Mount Everest, the thunder of Niagara Falls, the roar of a hurricane, the speed of Concorde, the authority of rulers, the control of the police, the love of money. These are all pictures of power: power in nature, power in people, power to create, power to destroy, power to fear and power to marvel at.

But there is also *spiritual* power and that's a power God wants us all to have. For the growing Christian the Holy Spirit is the power dimension.

Many people have difficulty in thinking about God the Holy Spirit as a person. People speak of the Spirit as 'it' rather than 'he'.

So, 'Who is the Holy Spirit?' Our first section of readings takes a look at that question. Get ready to discover him as the person without whom none of us can live the Christian life.

What is the Holy Spirit ready to do in our lives? Much more than we imagine... Section 2 is all about the way he satisfies and makes our lives more useful.

So the Holy Spirit wants to complete our lives, to make us whole people. But often we feel shy, hesitant and weak. That was just how Timothy felt before he discovered the power and help of the Holy Spirit. In section 3, our readings focus on Timothy.

Then in the final section we get a glimpse of what the Holy Spirit has done through his work in the early church, and what he is still able to do for us today.

Each set of readings (based on the NIV Bible though you can use other modern translations) is introduced by an article that includes more about the following theme. It also grapples with some of the knotty problems that come up in the Bible verses. Then the extras at the end of each series will help you delve a little more into the Bible's teaching on the Holy Spirit.

A QUIET PLACE

In a noisy, active world, it's often hard to be quiet, and stillness is one thing that really aids concentration. Here are some suggestions on how to get the most out of your time with God.

● *Find a quiet place.* Where can you be undisturbed by the phone, TV, or other people? Once you've found the best place, try to stick to it. For most, it will be at home; for some, a quiet office at work where they can spend a lunch hour or time after work.

● *Set aside a quiet time.* Some of us are best at the start of the day; others at the end. Work out the time – 10, 15, 20 minutes – when you can be quiet by yourself. Look on it as an appointment with God and try to keep it. Don't only read the Bible when you *feel* like it. It's good to fix the reading habit for *every* day. Read the Bible verses and think about them before looking at the notes. This way you will gain more.

● *Get a quiet mind.* Thoughts rush through our minds even when we are trying to settle down. You may find it helpful to have a pen and paper at hand to jot down wandering thoughts so that you can deal with them later. Allow some time to become aware of God's presence. Ask the Lord to help you *read, understand* and *apply* what you learn to your life.

PRAYER LINK

You will find it helpful to pray before and after you read the Bible. One of these two outlines might act as a guide:

1 Think of *sorry, thank you, please…*
- A *sorry* prayer – confessing your sin to God.
- A *thank you* prayer – thanking God for some blessing or answered prayer.
- A *please* prayer – asking the Lord to meet some particular need in your life.

2 Think of the word *ACTS*. That stands for:

Adoration – worship and praise God for who he is.

Confession – admitting failure and asking for forgiveness.

Thanksgiving – thanking God for what he has done.

Supplication – praying for other people or for yourself.

As you use one of these outlines your prayer life will begin to grow. Another booklet in this series, 'The PRAYER Principle' will also help as you seek to grow with Jesus.

GROWING WITH JESUS

It is normal for people to grow physically, emotionally and mentally. Growth is also an essential part of the Christian life and God wants us to grow spiritually. See, for example, Ephesians 2:21; Colossians 2:6, 7; 2 Thessalonians 1:3; 1 Peter 2:2; and 2 Peter 3:18.

GROWING UP WITH OTHERS

As we grow physically, we benefit from having other people around us. The same is true in the Christian life. We need to read and pray on our own, but it makes all the difference to meet with other Christians for sharing and encouragement. Are there *three* or *four* people you could perhaps meet with once a week, for about an hour, so that you can talk and pray together about what you have all been reading?

As you turn to the first article on the Holy Spirit – *God's power dimension for every Christian* – be ready to discover who he is.

the
power
dimension

Spotlight on

Invisible? Yes. But, nevertheless, very much alive and kicking! The Holy Spirit is the power dimension of our Christian life. His presence is vital if we want to be the kind of people God wants us to be.

the Holy Spirit

If we are to grow with Jesus, it will only come about with the help of the Holy Spirit. So, it's important to understand exactly who he is and what he can do for us. First and foremost, he's a person - the third person of the Trinity (Matthew 28:19; 2 Corinthians 13:14).

I think it helps to look at human history as a three-act play. God the Father, Son and Holy Spirit are all there at the beginning, waiting in the wings before the curtain goes up (Genesis 1:2). *Act 1* spans the time from the world's creation until the coming of Jesus. God the Father is the main character on stage, with the Son and Spirit making brief appearances. *Act 2* covers the Gospels and this time Jesus is centre stage. The ascension ushers in *Act 3* and the spotlight is on the Holy Spirit. That part of the play is still going on.

The Holy Spirit mustn't be thought of as 'packages of divine power' to be called on when needed. He is the person of God spiritually present in every believer. In the Old Testament (Psalm 104:30; Isaiah 40:13, 14) the Holy Spirit was active in the creation of the world and in revealing God's truth. Occasionally, he appeared to individuals for a special purpose (Exodus 31:1-3; Judges 6:34). Then Jesus came, and lived continually in the power of the Spirit (Luke 3:22 and 4:1, 14, 18). Jesus taught the disciples about the Holy Spirit, whom he promised to send to them after his ascension (*see* days 1 and 2).

EXECUTIVE DIRECTOR

Think of the Holy Spirit as the executive director of the Godhead, carrying out what God the Father plans for his world, his church and individuals. The Holy Spirit is always at work. He acts, speaks, guides, convicts, changes people, prompts and does the things that only a person can do. He is our heavenly senior partner in the Christian life. In fact, it's impossible to be a Christian at all *without* the Spirit. He is God's gift to every Christian, and to the church. But that's not all, he is also at work in the world. In this context, 'the world' refers to people who don't yet acknowledge God as God. So it's the task of the Spirit to show them their sin and to open their eyes to their need of the Saviour.

When anyone admits s/he is wrong and turns to Jesus confessing that he is the Saviour they need, then God gives the Holy Spirit to be their helper and friend for ever (*see* day 4).

CONSTANT COMPANION

It is not enough to know we have the Holy Spirit with us at the beginning of our Christian lives. We need to rely on him every day. Have a look at some great promises (Luke 11:13; John 7:37-39; Acts 2:38, 39 and 5:32). The Spirit can be our constant companion in the

the power dimension

the power dimension

Christian life and he will help us in all sorts of ways. For example:

• *He teaches us about God.* He reveals God's truth in the Bible. He helps us to understand it, obey it, and live it out. So it makes sense to pray for the help of the Spirit *before* you read each day.

• *The Holy Spirit wants to make us more like Jesus.* He wants to change our lives so that we are more loving, kind, gentle and patient. But there's a part for us to play as well. Repeatedly, you will find in the Bible readings and comments that God wants and expects us to obey him. So our readings are not just helpful hints on how to live each day, they call for a response. In loving obedience, we should follow God's leading and guidance day by day.

• *The Holy Spirit helps us to live and serve the Lord.* He will cause different abilities and gifts to develop as we grow with Jesus. Some of us, for example, will be good at caring for others; some teaching God's truth; some running an organisation, and some leadership.

HELPER

Some of God's gifts are given to help us tackle the ordinary every day things that need doing in the church (eg Romans 12:3-8). Some are given to help the leaders of the church (Ephesians 4:7, 11-13), and other spiritual gifts are given to help with tasks in the church that would be impossible without the help of the Holy Spirit - for example, healings, or special knowledge in helping other people. Paul says more about these spiritual gifts in 1 Corinthians, chapters 12 and 14.

All these gifts are the Holy Spirit's tools of the trade for the work of making the church effective in today's world.

• *The Holy Spirit wants the church to grow.* He is the Spirit who directs, strengthens and sustains every Christian in their work and witness so that the mission of the church can be fulfilled, and the church enlarged as more disciples are won for Jesus. We shall read all about this in one of the most exciting parts of the Bible - *The Acts of the Apostles.* As you read, remember that what the Holy Spirit did then, he goes on doing right now.

We are living in exciting days. All around the world Christians are discovering - and re-discovering - the Holy Spirit. He is alive! He is real! He is powerful! He is personal, and he lives in every Christian. He works in the world, and he directs the work of the church.

So, remember, it may be tough to be a Christian but we have the help and assistance of the Trinity all the time. *God the Father* loves me and reveals himself to me. *God the Son* saves me. And *God the Holy Spirit* is with me to help me know God, please God, serve God and glorify God in all I do.

That may sound an awful lot to understand all at once. I've tried to give an overall view so that you can keep your bearings as you study a bit of God's map for our lives each day, and as you begin, or continue, your Christian journey.

Spotlight on the Holy Spirit

Day 1
PROMISED BY JESUS
John 14:15-26

'Equal power for Big Three' might well be today's headline for this Bible reading. God the Father, Son and Holy Spirit are all at work and the great news is that their power is available to every Christian. There are some profound thoughts (v 23, for example). Don't worry if you can't grasp everything. Hang on to the truths you can.

Today's verses record some wonderful promises made by Jesus to his disciples. You may find it helpful to read them through several times. Most are about the Holy Spirit. He is called 'another Counsellor' or 'someone like Jesus brought alongside to help us on a permanent basis' (John 14:23, 26). He is a companion, counsellor, teacher, guide and friend for every Christian, and he's with us to help us grow like Jesus.

One thing John makes very clear is: only Christians can know the personal, permanent presence of the Holy Spirit in their lives. The world doesn't (see previous article - pages 5-7).

Prayer starter:
Loving the Lord and obeying the Spirit are the keys to 'knowing God'. Jesus loved and obeyed the Father and, what the Son did, his followers should aim to do as well.

Lord Jesus, thank you for your promised gift of the Holy Spirit. Help me to know his presence each day.

Day 2
TEACHER AND LEADER
John 15:26-16:15

It's strange for a mother to abandon her child. It's wrong for a driving instructor to desert an L-driver in the car. And the disciples must have thought it peculiar that Jesus said they would be better off without him (v 7)! However, Jesus was going to be their permanent representative in heaven, and the Holy Spirit was coming to be God's representative on earth. Jesus, unlike the Spirit, couldn't be everywhere at once. Three times he tells them what is going to happen (15:26; 16:8, 13).

- *He will testify about Jesus* (15:26). No one finds it easy to witness for Jesus to friends and neighbours. Sometimes we get mocked, or worse (16:1-4), but the Spirit will help. *How?*

- *He will show the world what's wrong* (16:8). Like a barrister in a law-court, the Spirit will present the evidence: we have sinned and are heading for judgement. When we feel guilty, the Holy Spirit may be pointing out something that needs to be changed.

- *He will teach us more about the Lord Jesus* (16:14). Jesus knows we can't learn everything at one go. So the Holy Spirit is with us to keep on teaching us about Jesus. Notice how the reading begins and ends with the Holy Spirit pointing a way to Jesus. Well, we will only grow with Jesus as we allow the Spirit room in our lives.

Prayer starter:
Lord Jesus, as the Holy Spirit tells me about you, help me also to tell the world.

the power dimension

Spotlight on the Holy Spirit

Day 3
GIVER OF NEW LIFE
John 3:1-17

the power dimension

There are not 'ordinary' Christians and 'born-again' Christians! *Every* Christian must be born again (v 3).

● *Nicodemus marvels at Jesus the teacher* (v 2). Nicodemus is a religious man, keeping the law learned in the Old Testament, but there is something missing. Jesus explains that new spiritual birth is the work of the Spirit of God, just as new physical birth is the gift of human parents. We may not fully understand, but it is as real as the wind blowing in the trees. (*Born of water and of the spirit may refer to the waters of human birth or of baptism.*) Spiritual birth is essential if we are to enter the kingdom and have spiritual understanding.

● *Jesus is amazed at Nicodemus the teacher* (v 10). Nicodemus didn't understand the difference between religion (*man reaching after God*) and Christianity (*God coming down in human form to man*). He needed to respond to Jesus to know this new birth. (See vs 11 and 12 for our response.) Regeneration (*being born again*) is God's work. We may not know the exact time or day when we were born again, but we can still be sure that we are spiritually alive for the Spirit doesn't leave us in doubt. If you are in doubt, then ask Jesus to forgive your sin, come into your life and give you the Holy Spirit.

Prayer starter:
Lord, help me to realise that what makes me a Christian is not what *I* do for you, but receiving what *you* have done for me.

Day 4
LASTING GUARANTEE
Ephesians 1:3-14

Are there times when you want to burst with excitement at some great news? That's how Paul felt when he wrote to the church at Ephesus (*situated in modern day Turkey*).

He was counting his blessings in Christ, and naming them one by one: God wanted him, brought him into his family, forgave his sins, taught him, etc. Take a look at all the blessings Paul sets out (v 4 onwards). They come to us through Jesus (v 3). If we are 'in Christ', then all these blessings are ours. But how do we know? That's where the Holy Spirit comes in (vs 13, 14). Paul uses *two* pictures:

● *A seal.* The Holy Spirit is like a seal (v 13). The seal is the legal stamp on a document certifying ownership of a house or land, etc. It proves the document is genuine. The Holy Spirit tells me that I belong to Jesus, that I am a real Christian and gives me the assurance that God won't break his promises.

● *A deposit.* The Holy Spirit is like a deposit (v 14). He is God's down-payment, assuring us more is to come. He is like an engagement ring, promising marriage. He is the present, ensuring the future.

Prayer starter:
The promises of God in Christ are assured and the future inheritance of seeing Jesus as he really is will be more glorious.

Thank you, Lord Jesus, for your marvellous blessings. Help me to enjoy them and not to spoil or neglect them.

Spotlight on the Holy Spirit

Day 5
GIVER OF WISDOM
Ephesians 1:15-23

We live in days when 'The New Age' claims we can develop our own inner resources of wisdom and understanding. But the New Testament teaches this is impossible except through the work of the Holy Spirit. Head knowledge about God is not enough. The Spirit makes it possible for us to enter into a relationship with God; to know him through personal experience.

The Holy Spirit gives new life. He gives assurance that this new life is ours, together with the help we need to grow as a Christian.

Because Paul wanted his friends to grow in their faith he prayed for them regularly (vs 15, 16). I wonder whether we always do the same? It thrilled Paul to think about the blessings available to Christians (*day 4*), and now he reflects on how we really can become effective spiritually. The key lies in verse 17 (compare Colossians 1:9). We need 'the Spirit of wisdom and revelation'. That could refer to our human spirit, but human understanding and reasoning are not enough. This is something that has to be a gift of the Holy Spirit: he makes Jesus known to us (*revelation*) and helps us to apply that knowledge to our lives (*wisdom*).

Prayer starter:
If you long to know God better, pray for the revelation and wisdom of the Spirit.

Day 6
HE MAKES THE DIFFERENCE!
Romans 8:1-17

Did you know you can't be a real Christian without the Holy Spirit (v 9)? Take a few minutes to read the passage again slowly. Did you notice that practically every verse is telling us something new? Consider:

● *What we do with the Spirit.* Paul describes living in the flesh and living in the spirit. One is defeat and death, the other is life and peace. So who is in charge of our lives? Are we allowing the flesh or the Holy Spirit to direct and control us?

● *What the Spirit does with us.* This is personal and practical. The Spirit assures us we are children of God. He leads our thoughts so we can talk with our heavenly Father in prayer, guides us about the future, strengthens us so that we can overcome temptation, and begins to make us more like Jesus.

A Christian is a person with two natures: one, selfish and sinful, the other, good and Christ-like. By starving the former, refusing to feed it with wrong thoughts, and, by feeding our spiritual nature with God's word, we shall grow more like our Lord Jesus. God wants to make us into better people.

Prayer starter:
Bring to the Lord those parts of your life that need changing. Invite the Holy Spirit to make you more like Jesus.

the power dimension

Spotlight on the Holy Spirit

True life experiences

Members of our church have different stories to tell about the Holy Spirit. One will speak of the love the Spirit gives, another will speak about the Spirit's help in witnessing at work. Yet another to the spirit of praise that bubbles up from within. The experiences differ, but the Spirit is the same. Take a look at:

- The testimony *of* Jesus. Make time to read Luke 3:21, 22 and Luke 4:1-21 (*especially* vs 1, 14, 18). You will find the Spirit asssuring Jesus, strengthening him, directing his work, etc.

- The testimony *to* Jesus. John the Baptist was right there (John 1:32-34). He saw what happened, and spoke of a marvellous promise to the church about the Holy Spirit baptising us. We shall discover that Christians haven't always agreed what the baptism of the Holy Spirit means. However, the New Testament teaches that this experience of the Holy Spirit is for *all* believers.

- The testimony *for* Jesus. What is your testimony about the Holy Spirit? Over the last week what have you discovered? In what ways have you become more aware of his presence and work? What promises are you claiming about the Holy Spirit in your life? Thank God for all that he has already done in you by the Holy Spirit.

Day 7
WONDERFUL GARDENER!
Galatians 5:13-26

Any garden – whether it be a window box or Kew Gardens – needs a gardener to get rid of the weeds and produce the flowers. Visitors may notice only the garden, and forget the gardener, but *he* is vital. So is our heavenly gardener – God – and he works through the Holy Spirit. There's no doubt that every garden needs:

- *The right soil.* 'Good lives' can't be grown in the wrong soil (*sinful nature*) but only in the Spirit. Notice the promise (vs 16-18). We are assured that we have the right soil, but we must use it.

- *The proper pruning.* Sometimes pruning has to be drastic. We have to cut out the desires of the flesh (v 16). Like suckers or weeds they take all the goodness from the plant. A horrible list is catalogued (vs 19-21). Don't be tempted to keep a few small plants – weeds have a habit of taking over!

- *The ripe fruit.* Obey the Spirit and he will produce a seven-fold crop of beautiful fruit. Because of their character there are those people who display some of this fruit more 'naturally' than others. However, the Spirit can grow all these fruits in the garden of our lives, but we have to do *our* part. See what verses 16, 18, 25 have to say about being led, and living by the Spirit.

Prayer starter:
(*Based on v 25.*) Lord Jesus, too often I go my own way, help me to obey the prompting of your Spirit today.

Spotlight on the Holy Spirit

Plug in for power

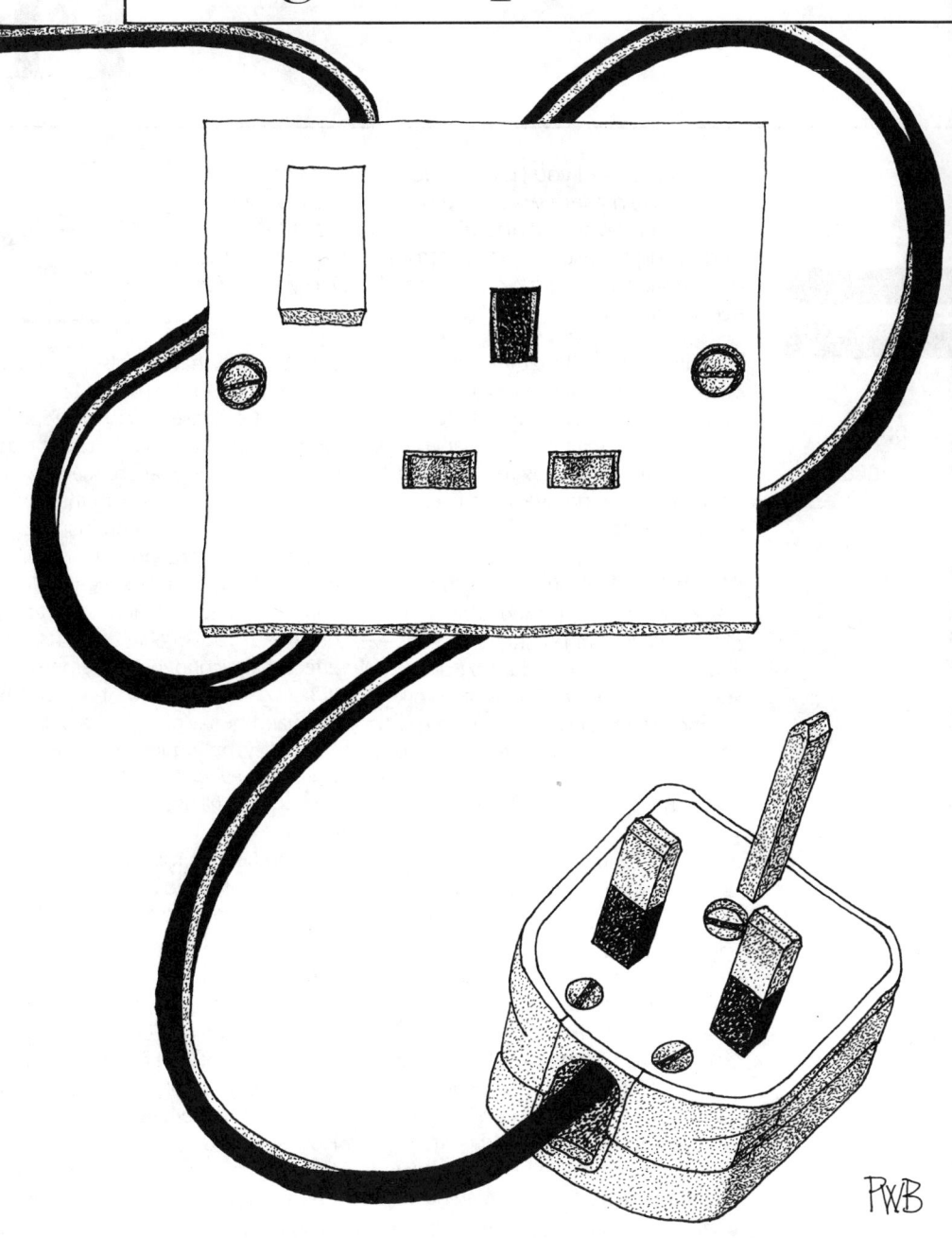

It's no good having power laid on if we aren't going to plug in. Trying on our own to win the battle against the devil, or struggling on our own to overcome the obstacles he places in our way is futile.

the power dimension

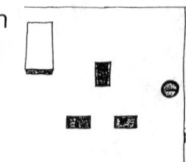

Do you ever feel you have made a mess of your Christian life? Or wish there was more help for you? Do you long to be more powerful and effective for Jesus? We are beginning to discover as we grow with Jesus that God has provided the gift and power of his Holy Spirit for every believer.

We sometimes feel that it is okay for other Christians but that it won't work for us. What we need to discover is that the Holy Spirit is as available to you and me as he was to Peter and Philip and other believers in the early church. We may ask:

What will the Holy Spirit do in my life?

We have already looked at how he gives new life and assurance, leads and speaks, produces the fruit of the Spirit in our lives, etc. This is the work of the Spirit about which every Christian agrees. But there are some aspects of the ministry of the Holy Spirit, that crop up in the readings, about which Christians have different views. For example:

● *The Holy Spirit baptises Christians.* There are at least half-a-dozen different views about this! The main debate is whether my baptism in the Spirit was when I first became a Christian, or later on when I realised my need of God's power to serve him. Is it a work of the Holy Spirit that happens consciously or unconsciously in our lives? I suggest you bear these comments in mind when you meet the word 'baptism' in the readings.

● *The Holy Spirit fills Christians.* On at least four occasions in our next series you will read that the disciples were filled with the Holy Spirit. But how do I know I am filled with the Spirit? Nowhere in the New Testament do we read an individual Christian saying the words, 'I am filled with the Spirit'.

What we do read (Ephesians 5:18) is that every Christian is to be filled with the Spirit. Literally it means: 'All of you must allow the Holy Spirit to go on filling you.' Paul contrasts the effect that alcohol has on a person – affecting his thinking, his speech, walk and behaviour generally. In the same way, he argues, the Holy Spirit will affect every part of us when we allow him to fill us and have complete control.

One effect of this will be that we have a heightened awareness of the power of God working through us. We shall be specially aware of the presence of Jesus.

● *The gift and gifts of the Holy Spirit.* Every Christian agrees that God gives the Holy Spirit. Every Christian also agrees that the Holy Spirit equips each Christian with different gifts of the Holy Spirit. But not everyone agrees that *all* the gifts are for today, and Christians also differ over the meaning of some gifts.

● *The gift of speaking in tongues.*

g in for power

Was it just the ability to speak in other recognised languages, not known to the speaker? Were they both heavenly and human languages? Did you have to 'speak in tongues' in order to prove to others that you were filled with the Holy Spirit?

Complete books have been written on all of the above topics. I have mentioned them to make sure you are aware of the issues.

But don't be discouraged. There is a great deal about the person, power, purpose and purity of the Holy Spirit on which there is complete agreement! He is also the Spirit of unity and we can know the unity and fellowship of the Spirit with other Christians even though we may not agree on *every* detail.

The Holy Spirit fills each Christian. He also acts powerfully when the members of a church or fellowship act together. The Holy Spirit directs and empowers the church. All this leads to our second question.

How should I respond to the Holy Spirit?

● *There are some things we mustn't do.* We are *not* to grieve or quench the Holy Spirit (Ephesians 4:30). We are *not* to disobey him.

Sin in our lives spoils our relationship with God. It stops the flow of God's power and leaves us weak and stunted in spiritual growth.

Rather, we must respond positively to the Holy Spirit. Growing with Jesus is about obeying some very practical New Testament commands. For example: I must turn from everything I know is wrong if I am to know the refreshing power of the Holy Spirit (Acts 3:19). I must long for more of his power in my life (John 7:37-39). I must obey what he tells me to do (Acts 5:32). I must ask the Lord to give me more and more of the Holy Spirit (Luke 11:13; Ephesians 5:18). It is God's work to go on giving the Spirit to every Christian but we must rely on and trust in his work and power (Galatians 3:1-3).

You may not understand everything about the Holy Spirit, but hold fast to what you do know. Just as a human body without breath is only a corpse, so the church without the indwelling Holy Spirit is dead.

As Jesus ministered in the power of the Spirit (Luke 3:21, 22; 4:1, 14, 18) so the church and every Christian must live and work in the power of the Spirit.

The following section of readings comes from the *Acts of the Apostles* – Luke's story of the early church. Meet Peter, Stephen and Philip and notice how the church grows at a fantastic rate. People are healed. Witness is bold. Persecution is fierce. The fellowship is strong. Behind all this is the Holy Spirit working in power. Discover the same power available to you.

the power dimension

Day 8
FIRE POWER
Acts 2:1-13

the power dimension

Strange, unique things can happen when the Spirit comes into our lives. The disciples heard the sound of a mighty wind (*a sign of God's power*). They saw the flames of fire (*a picture of God's holiness*). Each one was filled with the Spirit. Untrained men spoke in other tongues and began an international ministry. At least fifteen nationalities heard the good news of Jesus in their own language. Such a gift was for witness rather than assurance that they possessed the Holy Spirit in his fullness.

The disciples knew the coming of the Holy Spirit because they were obedient. God had told them to wait in the city (Luke 24:49). There they had witnessed that Jesus was alive (Acts 1:8) and now their misery and despair is being replaced with the power, exhilaration and joy of knowing the Holy Spirit at work through them.

Pentecost – a major Jewish feast – marked the giving of the law to Moses. It was also the middle of three annual Jewish harvest festivals. The gift of the Spirit brought to Pentecost a new meaning. The Spirit would help every Christian to keep God's law, and he would produce the spiritual harvest that Jesus had spoken about (Matthew 28:19, 20).

Prayer starter:
The Holy Spirit is given to make us bold and strong. To give us the power to communicate the good news about Jesus to all nations.

Day 9
OBEDIENCE AND POWER
Acts 4:1-22

Do you sometimes feel fearful and tongue-tied when the opportunity is there to speak about your faith? Do you tell yourself it would all be different if you had been to Bible College? Do you think it was easier for Peter?

Remember he once boasted he would never let Jesus down. Yet he did. Now, with John, he stands up to the religious and military leaders.

The Sanhedrin was made up of 71 Sadducees, chaired by the high priest. These men, who earlier had tried Jesus, were wealthy aristocrats who didn't believe in the resurrection. Unlike the Sadducees, Peter had had no official theological college training, yet he knew that Jesus was alive.

Peter had told the crowd that his power came from Jesus (3:12). And he said the same after his arrest (4:10).

Both Peter and John grew spiritually as they made up their minds to do what Jesus told them, rather than listen to the orders of the religious leaders.

Thought provoker:
Do you face the choice of obeying men, rather than Jesus? Remember, Peter was an effective witness, with the help of the Holy Spirit, *because* he was an obedient witness. See the promise in Acts 5:32 – God gives the Holy Spirit to all who obey him. *Will you?*

Plug in for power

Day 10
PRAYER POWER
Acts 4:23-31

In January 1949, a young man (18), an apprentice blacksmith, was praying with a group of believers on the Isle of Lewis in the Hebrides. Today's scripture reading was open before them.

When they claimed the power of God, the place literally shook.

The Holy Spirit descended on them. Pots and pans fell. People were converted. A spiritual revival began.

The early church grew *because* it prayed. Peter and John, in trouble for witnessing, returned to their fellowship and prayed a powerful prayer. They acknowledged that God is creator, and therefore acts; that he is revealer through the Holy Spirit and the Scriptures, and therefore speaks; that he is sovereign Lord and Saviour, and therefore miraculously saves his people. Most of the prayer praises God. Only at the end do they ask that God will protect and empower them. Some powerful things happen (v 31).

Prayer starter:
Most of us need encouragement to pray for ourselves, our church and fellowship. Praise God for what he has done in your life and, with renewed confidence, release the power of God's Spirit through prayer.

Why not arrange to meet with friends? Plan a time to pray with others and share together all that the Lord has done.

Day 11
POWER FOR SOLUTIONS
Acts 6:1-7

Every growing church has problems. The early church was no exception – the Grecian Jews felt their widows were neglected. Here was a practical, racial and cultural problem. But they had the Holy Spirit to guide them. Note what the leaders did.

● *They set out their priorities* (v 4). The word 'ministry' is used (vs 2, 4). The ministry of serving tables and preaching are both important, but prayer and preaching had to come first for the apostles. They knew that gettting too caught up in administration could mean their praying and preaching would suffer.

● *The church selected special people to handle this new situation.* Those chosen had little experience but were godly and Spirit-filled men (vs 3-6). The apostles authorise their ministries and they are ready to grow in leadership and service.

Sometimes when there are problems in a church, people leave. But what was the result here (v 7)? *More* people joined the church because the Holy Spirit helped the leaders handle the problem in the right way.

Prayer starter:
Are there people who should be set free for service in your church? In quietness, bring this, and any problems in your fellowship, to the Lord. Ask the Holy Spirit to show you the right way to solve them. Thank him that he has the power to do this.

the power dimension

Plug in for power

the power dimension

Day 12
POWER TO PREACH
Acts 8:4-25

Instead of growing with Jesus, through the Spirit's help, everything now seemed to be going wrong. Stephen had been martyred. Saul was stirring up trouble. The church members had been scattered and the leaders were locked in Jerusalem. Yet, great things were about to happen. The power of the Spirit was going to be at work through Philip's evangelistic preaching and healing. The result: great joy.

Often when God is at work by his Spirit, others try to copy and counterfeit what is happening (vs 9-13, 18-24). The same is true today. We have many new counterfeit religious movements – especially the New Age – claiming to satisfy the spiritual hunger in people. How should we be responding to these situations?

● *Don't be shy.* Ask for help from other Christians. Peter and John – more experienced leaders – gave their advice. In that way, you, and the work will grow in Jesus.

● *Be sincere.* The apostles told Simon he had responded to the good news with his head, but not with his heart and will (v 21). He still had to repent.

● *Expect God to work in unexpected places.* The leaders confirmed that the Samaritans – outcasts as far as Jews were concerned – had received the gospel. Hands were laid on them for assurance, welcome and blessing.

Prayer starter:
Holy Spirit, help me to know what is true or false in all I find in today's world.

Day 13
POWER TO TEACH
Acts 8:26-40

Most of us find it hard to speak about Jesus. But the Holy Spirit who helped Philip is there for us.

In 'day 12' we saw the good news of Jesus being preached in a Samaritan city. Now, Philip is sharing the same message with the Ethiopian, who was the queen's household treasurer. Different people, different race, rank and religion, but the message is the same.

The road from Jerusalem to Gaza and on to Egypt was the M1 of the day. It was desert, but not deserted. It can't have been easy for Philip to approach this African sitting in his chariot but he had learned that it is wise to obey when prompted by the Spirit. Jesus learned obedience (Hebrews 5:8). So did Philip. If we think about the results, then it ought to spur us on. We can trust the Holy Spirit to lead us clearly (vs 26, 29, 39). We can be sure that he is there before us, preparing the way (*the Ethiopian was already reading the Old Testament and asked for help*) and will guide us in what we should say (v 35).

Prayer starter:
The Ethiopian probably returned to establish a church in his country. Philip, filled with great joy, was encouraged to go forward in his service for the Lord.

Lord Jesus, help me to listen to the Holy Spirit so that I hear and obey his promptings.

Plug in for power

Day 14
POWER OF THE SPIRIT
Acts 11:1-18

When God does new things by his Spirit, the church doesn't always find it easy to accept what's happening. The Holy Spirit may be bringing changes to the worship, fellowship or teaching in your church. Perhaps some find it hard to accept, because – 'We've always done it this way!'

It was hard for Peter, at first. The thought that a Gentile – Cornelius – could actually become a Christian and receive the Holy Spirit was abhorrent to a Jew. Gentiles were 'unclean' (v 8). For us, we may assume that people with a very different background can't become Christians – eg the man who spends all his time in the pub or is rotten to his wife. Well…

It took four hammer blows to break Peter's prejudice' (*Dr John Stott*). There was the divine vision (10:11); command (10:13-16); preparation (10:17); and action (10:23ff). All of which led Peter to understand that God was doing something new and exciting.

This break-through shows that the unity of the church should be based on the message of the good news, and the work of the Spirit, *not* on culture and tradition. A whole new world has been opened up so that the good news of Jesus could eventually be brought to us.

Prayer starter:
What new things is the Spirit wanting to do in your life and fellowship? Ask for his power to deal with any resistance that is holding things back.

Hot or cold?

The radiators in our house were sometimes hot and then cold, yet we hadn't fiddled with the time clock or the dials. We telephoned the plumber and explained. 'Ah,' he said, 'classic symptoms of pump failure.' It turned out that we'd got sludge in the system. The power was there, but it wasn't getting through to where it was needed.

PARTNERSHIP It can be like that in the Christian life. It may be the sludge of prejudice, fear, unbelief or disobedience that blocks the power supply and we blow hot and cold as Christians. We need to work in partnership with the Spirit.

Look back to Acts 1:8 and recall that the church had been established in Jerusalem and had then spread to Judea, Samaria and to the Gentile world. Of course, the Holy Spirit didn't do all this alone. He worked in partnership with people. Christians were constantly being filled with the Holy Spirit.

TAKE NOTE Allow the Holy Spirit to go on filling you (Ephesians 5:18).

Spend some time allowing the Holy Spirit to point out whether there are any spiritual blockages in your life. Confess them. Ask God to deal with them and invite the Holy Spirit to fill and use your life again.

extra

Plug in for power

Jesus made it plain that becoming a Christian means becoming a new person. We are reborn as God's children and adopted into a new family. Our inheritance waits for us in heaven.

A new person

'God looks for better men not better methods.' God works through people, and even though most of us feel unworthy, unqualified and unable, the Holy Spirit can change all that. He can equip us for God's service. Our next series of readings prove the truth of this.

You may be a very young Christian starting out at work. You may be a young mum struggling with a young family. You may have been a member of the church for many years. You might have just started a new job in the fellowship. You may even be the pastor! As we turn our attention to the life and ministry of Timothy, there will be something relevant for everyone.

Timothy lived at Lystra. It was there he first met Paul, heard the good news of Jesus and was converted. He had known the Scriptures from early childhood but now they came alive in a new way.

I've known that to be true for lots of Christians. They have faithfully read the Bible, but then discovered more about the power of the Spirit. The Bible comes alive in a new way, and they grow with Jesus again.

We discover more about Timothy and his family (Acts 16:1; 2 Timothy 1:5). He travelled with Paul. Gradually his responsibilities increased and he was appointed pastor of the church at Ephesus. You may have been given new responsibilities in your church and fellowship. Like Timothy, you could feel shy and nervous about taking these on. Perhaps, you don't see yourself as a natural leader, or maybe, even feel that you are too young for the job.

GREAT EXPECTATIONS

You might find that other people's expectations for you are great. Timothy himself was expected to stand up for the truth of the gospel, to set fellow Christians a good example, to care for other Christians, to make sure that he himself was spiritually on top form, to look out for other people to become leaders. And he was doing all this at a time when people were not really interested in the church and the Christian message. A bit like today? Timothy probably found it all as tough an assignment as we do. But he coped and through the power of the Holy Spirit, grew with Jesus.

● *He drew spiritual strength from God's word.* The Bible teaches us about the Holy Spirit. The Holy Spirit inspired those who originally wrote, and makes clear its meaning to us who read it today. The Holy Spirit and the Holy Scriptures go hand in hand; both the Spirit and the Scriptures point to Jesus. As someone once said: If you use the Bible without the Spirit, you will dry up. If you rely on the Spirit without the Scriptures, you will blow up. But if you rely on the Scriptures *and* the Spirit, you will grow up.

● *He was encouraged to fan the Spirit*

the power dimension

the power dimension

into flame. He wasn't to assume the Holy Spirit would do it all. There is a partnership. The Christian shouldn't act without the Spirit. In turn, the Spirit usually doesn't act without the Christian. When we are in step with the Spirit, there is effective action.

• *He was obedient.* Obedience is the key to effective Christian living. Holiness of life will affect our actions, words, thoughts, reactions, relationships, etc. So we need to be pure, holy and obedient in all these very 'down to earth' areas if we want to know the power of the Spirit. The Spirit is also the Spirit of Truth. As we believe the truth, live it out, so we shall know his power.

NOT ON YOUR OWN

A few months ago, I stood with a fellowship group for a simple communion service. Our hostess had placed a cup of wine and a freshly baked loaf of bread on the table, and also a very large bunch of full-grown grapes. Each grape belonged to a little cluster around it, and yet each grape was personally joined to the stem and to the vine. Each grape belonged to a small group, but was nourished by the vine. That should be true for us. We can be encouraged by other Christians in the fellowship of the Spirit, but we need to draw our spiritual life directly from the Lord Jesus himself.

When that happens we shall experience the new life that the Spirit gives, and like Timothy shall be new people in the service of the Master.

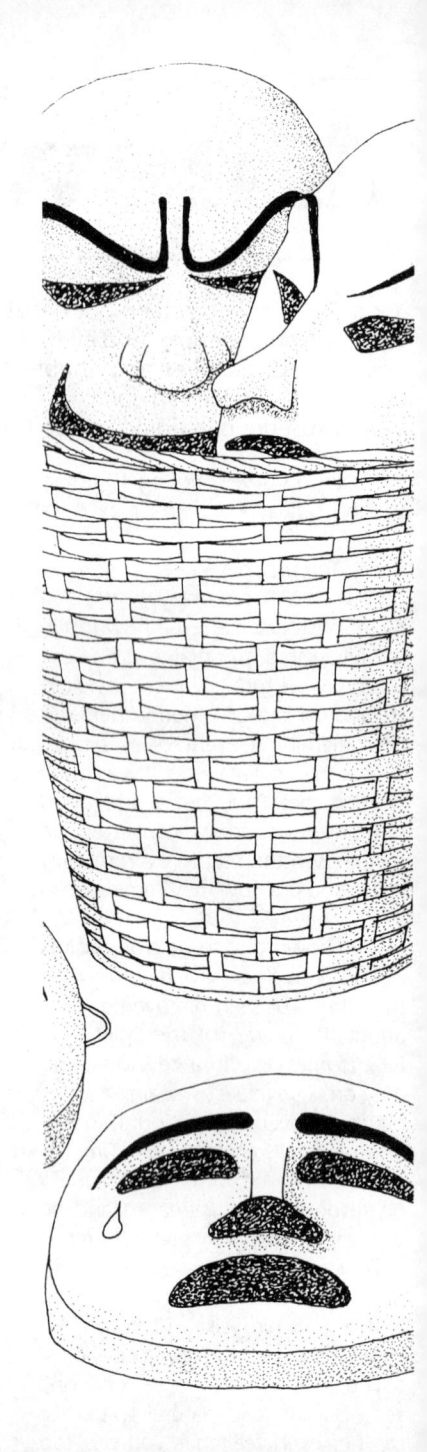

A new person

Day 15
NO NEED TO BE SHY
2 Timothy 1:1-7

Sometimes when family and friends expect too much from us, we hold back. We become hesitant. Timothy was rather like that. Although he had considerable leadership responsibility, he regarded himself as a natural No 2. Yet he had been specially appointed to his task. He already knew he possessed the Holy Spirit. But, still, he was hesitant and needed encouragement, and reminding of the power available to him (v 6). Note:

- *The Holy Spirit is not a spirit of fear* (v 7; Romans 8:15). When we are afraid our fear comes from Satan or our human spirit. But help is at hand.
- *Our every need can be provided.* Paul describes the Spirit in three ways (v 7) – each thought is important. Timothy needed courage and power for his ministry, self-discipline in his life, and love towards those he served. And he got what he needed!
- *Our spiritual fire calls for some attention* (v 6). When you stir up a fire, you open it up to the air (*the wind of the spirit*), rake out all the dead ash (*get rid of the muck*), and put on more fuel (*build it up with the truth of God*). What about the fire in your own heart and life? Do you find Luke 24:32 is true, or do you need to fan the life of the Spirit into flame again?

Prayer starter:
'Come, Holy Ghost, our souls inspire. And lighten with celestial fire.'

Day 16
NO NEED TO BE ASHAMED
2 Timothy 1:8-14

Are you sometimes ashamed of the name of Jesus, the gospel and your fellow Christians? We are reminded that there is no need for this once we have fanned the Holy Spirit into activity. Paul and Onesiphorus had proved this for themselves (vs 12, 16). But there's more:

We must be willing to suffer (v 8), take a look at our own lifestyle (v 9) and hold on to what we believe (v 12). We are not to be ashamed of being Christians in today's tough and unbelieving world. It's all part of growing with Jesus.

If you feel God is asking a lot *from* you, remember, he has given a great deal more *to* you. Take time to think about the grace of God (v 9) that embraces all his loving provision for every situation.

In fact, Paul likens the good news to a very costly treasure (v 14) that is handed down from generations. Sometimes, such heirlooms are hidden away and forgotten. But Timothy is to make sure he guards and uses his inheritance through Jesus.

As you go into today/tomorrow, don't forget that the Holy Spirit will help you speak with confidence about your faith in Jesus.

Prayer starter:
Ask yourself, 'Do I ever feel fearful in speaking about Jesus?' What help has today's reading given?

the power dimension

A new person

the power dimension

Day 17
READY FOR ANYTHING
2 Timothy 2:1-13

In the musical, 'Oliver', Oliver Twist's song went like this: 'I'd do anything for you…' and the reply of the gang – 'Anthing?' There may be times when we feel the Lord is asking the same of us – 'Anything?' Paul outlines five steps that will make it possible to be ready for anything.

● *Receive* the grace of Christ (v 1). Because of God's love and power we can each one be strong spiritually, and stand firm in the faith when others around may be weak and unsure.

● *Relay* the truth to other people (v 2). We can pass on what we have discovered by our testimony, lending a book or tape, encouraging a young Christian, teaching. If it is good enough to keep, then pass it on to others!

● *Resist* the temptations in Christian service (vs 3-6). These verses are full of pictures. Each has its own purpose and its pitfalls – such as getting sidetracked, breaking God's rules for holy living, being lazy. How might these dangers face you?

● *Reflect* on what you have been taught (v 7). Thinking (*or meditation*) is the means by which we feed our souls from God's word and become strong.

● *Remember* Jesus is alive and can be trusted (vs 8-13). So keep your eyes on him.

Prayer starter:
Lord Jesus, help me to fulfil your purpose for my life.

Day 18
APPROVED BY GOD
2 Timothy 2:14-19

Life is full of words. Some hurt. Some help. We have to learn to handle them if we want God's approval and grow with Jesus.

For Timothy, the teacher and pastor, there was clear advice (vs 14, 16-18). People can be hurt by quarrelling over words. Instead, Timothy was to remind his congregation about the good things of the gospel.

We shouldn't despise being told what we already know or always be looking for something new. We all need to be reminded about the basics of the Christian faith.

One of the dangers facing busy Christians is the quick read of the Bible. Paul reminds us that if we are going to be approved by God (v 15), then we have to take time and trouble in reading, studying, understanding and applying what we read in the Bible. That way we shall please not only ourselves, but also our Heavenly Master.

We shall be people who win God's approval when we use words that help other people, rather than hurting them.

Prayer starter:
'Set a guard over my mouth, O Lord; keep watch over the door of my lips' (Psalm 141:3).

A new person

Day 19
ON SPECIAL SERVICE
2 Timothy 2:20-26

On special occasions we bring out the best china – 'the Sunday best' (*for 'noble use'*). The rest, in use every day, becomes a bit tarnished and the cracks show (*'ignoble'*). Paul uses this picture to encourage us to aim at serving the Lord in such a way that the ordinary becomes special in the Lord's service. If we are to be on special service for God, then we need to be in pristine condition, always clean and ready for the next job. That's why Paul urges Timothy to turn away from anything and everything that would spoil his life and go after the things that would make it more useful to God.

What Paul wrote still applies today. What do you look at in the papers or on the station bookstall? What do you turn off on TV when others are around? How do you react to dirty jokes in the office? How do you respond when unfairly criticised – whether at work or in your family? Paul's aim is that we should be more like Jesus in a sinful world.

Being on special service affects how we talk with those who have different views on religion (vs 24-26). Do we argue, shout, get hot under the collar? All that is out of place for the Christian. According to Paul, we should be more concerned to win the person than win the argument.

Prayer starter:
Lord, help me always to be ready to do your will, to serve you whatever the task on hand.

Day 20
ON SOLID GROUND
2 Timothy 3:10-17

What can we be sure about these days? Who can we trust? Why do people let us down? What can we really rely on? Timothy's world – like ours – was drifting away from God's standards, so Paul urges him, and us: to continue in God's word (v 14). That involves:

● *going on* reading the Bible. Instead of only reading it when we feel like it, we have to give it a high priorty in life.

● *understanding* the purpose of the Bible. It tells about the way of salvation, and equips us for everything we have to do (vs 16, 17).

● *trusting* the reliability of the Bible. God breathed out the Scriptures by the Holy Spirit, so that what men wrote, God also wrote (2 Peter 1:20, 21; 1 Corinthians 2:1-14).

I can't promise you an easy life. But when storms rage we can be sure of being on solid ground (vs 10-13). Paul didn't hide the difficulties he had faced. Yet, he could testify to the Lord's faithfulness in bringing him through everything.

You may feel rocked by life – redundancy, marriage break-up, problems with the children, sudden troubles or unexpected changes. Whatever our situation, we are on solid ground with God's word.

Prayer starter:
Father help us to hold fast to the hope you have given us in Jesus.

the power dimension

A new person

No holding back

If you are thinking, I want to be a new person but I'm afraid... shy... inexperienced... tempted, then take another look at the key verse in Paul's letter to Timothy. 'God did not give us a spirit of timidity, but a spirit of power, of love and of self-discipline? (1:7). Then take time to apply that truth to the things that hold you back.

AFRAID? What are you afraid about? A person? Something in the future? Some unconfessed sin from the past, illness or death? Remember, it is the work of the Holy Spirit to replace fear with trust. In your heart and mind, allow him to do just that.

SHY? Whatever the situation, ask the Holy Spirit to take away the shyness, and give you boldness for today.

INEXPERIENCED? You feel inexperienced for Christian service. You have to lead the prayers at church, or read the lesson, or teach a class of children. There is a new work that you have just taken on. Why not ask two or three friends to pray with you, and for you, that you might know the wisdom and help of the Holy Spirit?

TEMPTED? You are battling with temptation, ask the Holy Spirit to remind you of the example of Jesus, and give you a hatred of sin and a desire for holiness.

Day 21
PRIZE WINNERS
2 Timothy 4:1-8

It is never going to be easy to serve the Lord (vs 3, 4). People only want to hear what *they* want to hear. They don't want to know what God says, just to have their own desires and fancies affirmed. But we can *all* be prize-winners, rather than failures. God has given the Holy Spirit to help us in our task. If you feel overwhelmed and daunted, remember 'our competence comes from God' (2 Corinthians 3:1-6).

It is not just skills and abilities that matter, but also the help which the Spirit gives. We still need to be level-headed, and face hardships (v 5). But it's sticking at the task God has given us (v 2) – whatever the conditions – that will help us to become prize-winners (vs 6-8).

Older and more mature Christians, like Paul, have a special ministry here. They can encourage those who are finding the going hard.

Paul knows that for him death is near. He picks up some of the pictures used already in 2:3-5 (*day 17*) and applies them to himself. Excited about the reward in glory, he is unafraid of death, because he knows what the Lord has in store for him. Serving the Lord in the power of the Spirit won't save us from 'blood, toil, sweat and tears', but we can be spurred on by all that God has promised.

Prayer starter:
Lord, help me not to be afraid of the future and of death, but to look forward to the prize you have in store for me.

extra

A new person

New horizons

Bored with things at the moment? Feel stagnant as a Christian? Well, maybe you need to pick up a 'stone' and throw it into the pool of faith, then watch for the results.

the power dimension

If you have stood and watched children throwing stones into a pond, you can picture the ripples spreading out to the edges. In the same way, as the early church shared the good news of Jesus at the centre (*Jerusalem*) so the ripples began to move outwards to the rest of the world. They couldn't have done this without the help of the Holy Spirit.

The good news, that looked at first as if it was just for the Jews, was in fact to be shared with the rest of the world, through the work of the Holy Spirit and the church.

There have been times in history when the church hasn't been bothered about telling people about Jesus. Times when Christians were more concerned with their own comfort than bringing people into God's family. But things have moved forward in the last one hundred and fifty years. Many of our modern day missions started during that time: Scripture Union in 1879; YWAM and Tear Fund in the last twenty-five years. Today, the church is alive, thriving in places such as Russia, China and Albania, that once were completely closed to the gospel. It's growing, too, in Latin America, Africa and the Far East.

But perhaps it's not enough to think of the growth of mission - and new horizons - like a stone being thrown into the pond. Sometimes, it's more like a busy railway junction. Though it's not just a matter of people being sent east to tell others, but of others coming to the west from places such as India, Nigeria and Chile, for the same reason.

FOLLOW THE LEADER

Mission is happening in a complex and confusing world. Alongside the Christian faith are a whole host of established world religions, and many new religious movements. In this country alone, the church has counted about 200. The main challenges to the spread of the Christian faith are from Islam and the New Age movement. Many competing voices distract people's attention, and seek to win their hearts and minds. More than ever, we need the guidance, power and work of the Holy Spirit.

- *How he works:* God and the Holy Spirit are at work in many different ways. He is constantly surprising us. But, for now, think about how he works through:

- *the witness of Christians* - both through the leaders and through ordinary members. As they were obedient to Jesus, so the early church was given a boldness to witness to others about Jesus. The theme of boldness is one to watch for in our next series of readings.

- *the word of God.* It is essential to know what God is saying to us and to be sure of what we believe, because we live in an age when most people

New horizons

don't understand what Christians believe. There's a need for teaching and preaching to go on in every day living not only in our churches, but in conversation, through literature, tapes, etc.

- *the unexpected.* The Holy Spirit also works through dramatic ways - maybe a healing, a miracle, etc. They are meant to assure us that God is alive and able to change people today.

- *Who he uses:* God the Holy Spirit works through people - such as Peter, John, Philip and Paul. But more often it's through the ordinary church member who is ready and willing to share the good news about Jesus.

'But I can't' people exclaim. Whatever the reason or excuse, we should pray for others, that they might find faith in Jesus. We can pray for those we know who are spreading the good news, for the outreach work of our churches and fellowships. We can write letters and use the phone.

Through us, horizons can be extended. Think of the people *your* life touches. If you are especially burdened for some to know Jesus, why not make a list? It may be two or three names - some in your family, a neighbour, someone you meet every day. Perhaps you find yourself burdened for one part of the world and could begin to pray for the churches there.

If your church supports various missions, you could begin to take their magazine, start to give money towards the work. Maybe there are stirrings in your life, indicating that you should be thinking and planning to change your job because God is calling you to be involved in sharing the good news in a bigger or full-time way?

For all of us, there can, and should be, new horizons.

Useful Addresses

TEAR Fund
100 Church Road
Teddington
Middlesex
TW11 8QE

Scripture Union
130 City Road
London
EC1V 2NJ

Bible Society
Stonehill Green
Westlea
Swindon
Wiltshire
SN5 7DG

Operation Mobilisation
The Quinta
Weston Rhyn
Oswestry
Shropshire
SY10 7LT

the
power
dimension

Day 22
WITNESSES FOR JESUS
Acts 1:1-11

the power dimension

Wouldn't it be fascinating to have a Gospel written to you personally, answering all your questions? But have you noticed that the *Gospel of Luke* and the *Acts of the Apostles* are both addressed to Theophilus (*Lover of God*)? He may have been an individual but it could be a title to describe *every* Christian.

Like us, the disciples were full of questions about the future. Jesus didn't answer them all, but made it clear that the coming of the kingdom was possible following his death, resurrection and ascension together with the coming of the Holy Spirit. As a result, every believer would:

- *receive power* (v 8). The promised Holy Spirit would be with us always to strengthen and show us how to be like Jesus.
- *be chosen* (v 8). We are representatives and witnesses for Jesus. It's an honour to be able to tell others about our personal knowledge of Jesus. That will include not only our up-to-date testimony, but also the facts about Jesus – his sufferings, death, resurrection, ascension and return.
- *spread the word*. If you get discouraged, consider how far the church has spread, and how it has survived throughout history. For this to happen, Christians have to be baptised, filled with the spirit and obedient to God.

Prayer starter:
Lord Jesus, help me to spread your good news where I live and work.

Day 23
GOOD NEWS FOR ALL
Acts 10:34-48

Whatever our background, God has no favourites. Christians can come from every race, nationality and class. The good news is for *all*. In your mind, do you assume that certain people could never become Christians? Well, consider Cornelius!

We've already heard Peter's account of what happened to him and his family (*day 14*). Today we return to the story at a point when Peter has just grasped that the good news is for all. On this special occasion the gift of the Holy Spirit was poured out on Gentiles *as well as* Jews. Cornelius and his household begin to speak in tongues (v 46).

Not every spiritual experience will be like this. But what is essential, however, is that every believer has been baptised in water, baptised in the Spirit, knows they are in Christ, and responds to everything the Holy Spirit does.

Prayer starter:
Sometimes we forget that God can work powerfully in people who live close by – our family, neighbours, friends at work or school.

Lord, please forgive me for thinking you won't work in the lives of people I meet every day. Fill me with your Spirit so that through what I say and do I can be a good witness for Jesus.

New horizons

Day 24
WITNESS BY EXAMPLE
Acts 2:42-47

What is your church like? Today, we read of the kind of fellowship I think we would all want to belong to!

Everyone agrees together in heart and mind. They meet with one another for worship and for fellowship in smaller groups. They are generous, giving and sharing their belongings. Their devotion and praise for God leads to others being added to the church. The people around really sense the presence of Jesus and the witness of the church members permeates throughout the neighbourhood (v 47).

Think about the witness of one member in particular – Barnabas. His name means 'Son of encouragement'. Humble and generous, he welcomed Paul as a young Christian when others were frightened of the former Jewish rabbi.

In our churches today, there are some lovely 'Barnabas types' – both men and women who go out of their way to welcome and encourage, and generally do all they can to help others grow strong and active for Jesus. Words, attitudes, character all matter, but ultimately it is the Holy Spirit dwelling in every Christian who makes the difference (4:31). The Spirit helps us witness boldly and changes our attitudes. As he produces qualities such as humility, generosity, love for others, the church grows and Christians keep on growing with Jesus.

Day 25
WITNESS BY OBEDIENCE
Acts 5:17-41

We are often involved in spiritual conflict. It may be the tussle between what God wants and what we want. It may be conflict between our Christian faith and the demands of an ungodly boss at work. It may be between resisting temptation or giving in when we are alone.

Peter and John's teaching and the healing of the man who couldn't walk produced conflict. The Sanhedrin were furious, fearful and jealous. They ordered Peter and John to be flogged.

Not many of us will be called upon to face conflict that brutal – though mockery or persistent hostility for our faith can be just as painful. It can cause us to keep quiet and give up. But in the face of opposition, the apostles obeyed. They obeyed the angel's command (vs 20, 21). They disobeyed the council's order (v 28). The result: the good news was preached. They knew the presence of the Holy Spirit (vs 31, 32). They were able to praise the Lord for the honour of suffering for Jesus (vs 41, 42). Their obedience to God, with the help of the Spirit, made them even more powerful than the Sanhedrin. So we can be sure that whatever God asks us to do for him – it's possible, with the power of the Spirit.

Prayer starter:
Lord, help me to obey you, not only when it is easy, but also when it is tough.

the power dimension

New horizons

Day 26
WITNESS BY WORD
Acts 6:8-15

the power dimension

Some Christians have a really tough time at home, college or work. They are denied promotion, mocked in public and treated unfairly. In some countries, there have been those who have literally faced the possibility of death.

Stephen was the first Christian to die for his faith. His attackers were furious because of what he had to say. He seemed to strike at the very heart of all they held sacred and precious. They failed to understand that Jesus had come to fulfil the Law, not to destroy it (John 2:19; Matthew 5:17).

If we live among Jewish neighbours, then we need to understand how they feel about their faith before we speak to them about Jesus. We should seek to help them find fulfilment, as Jews, in Jesus the promised Messiah.

Those who persecuted Stephen were driven by the spirit of jealousy, which, left unchecked, progressed to slander and violence. Stephen was upheld by the spirit of Jesus. Although his life ended prematurely it was not a waste. Watching his stoning was Saul of Tarsus (Acts 8:1). Stephen's witness – what he said (*his words*) and what he did (*his life*) – was to have a profound effect on Saul, later named Paul.

Prayer starter:
Never think you waste your life when you allow the Holy Spirit to take control.

Day 27
WITNESSING BY LOVE
Acts 9:32-43

Time spent loving and caring for others in need is time well used. However busy Peter was as leader of the church, he had time – and opportunity – to witness by his love. There are four little episodes in today's reading. Notice:

- *Peter the visitor* (v 32). A fisherman by trade, but a shepherd of people by calling. Like Peter, are there people you could encourage with a loving word today?

- *Praying for healing* (v 34). God must have made it clear that he was going to heal Aeneas. The sick people we know may not always be healed but that shouldn't stop us showing our love by praying for them.

- *In on a miracle* (v 40). Twelve miles away at Joppa, Dorcas had just died. Peter was sent for. Love was shown in taking time to visit, appreciating everything she had made, and, in this case, praying for her restoration to life.

- *A time of restoration* (v 43). Those who love need to be loved themselves. Do we have the gift and opportunity to offer hospitality to others?

Thought provoker:
Read Romans 5:6-8 and Galatians 5:22. As we allow the Holy Spirit to pour God's love into our hearts so we shall be able to love others through hospitality, encouragement, healing and comfort. What are the 'blocks' in our lives that hinder us from reflecting that love to others?

New horizons

Day 28
KEEPING GOING
Acts 28:16-31

Are there times when you feel like giving up? You are tired. You have done your share. You are discouraged. Things are hard. I suspect that every Christian feels that way at times. But there was no stopping this man, Paul!

Two or three days after the trauma of the sea voyage (*4-5 months in all*), he is again witnessing about the kingdom of God and the good news of Jesus.

He meets fellow Jews, partly to share the good news about Jesus and partly to put the record straight about himself. Verse 31 is a great summary verse. But what happened next? Did Paul stop? No!

Released, he resumes his travels, until he is rearrested, tried, condemned and executed in AD 64. But what kept him going? He told the church of Rome the secret. There were three things:

- He was *convinced* the gospel could change lives (Romans 1:16).
- He was *burdened* that his fellow Jews should be saved (Romans 10:1).
- He was *ambitious* to tell those who had never heard the good news about Jesus (Romans 15:20).

Prayer starter:
And what keeps us going? Who will go on helping us to grow with Jesus? We have the same power of the Holy Spirit. So are there more people and places where we should be sharing the news about Jesus? Pray that God will give you the boldness to keep growing with him *and* going for him.

That bit more...

You might well be feeling a sense of 'well, I've finished', but why not give 'the power dimension' just that bit more of your time and...

DISCOVER There's no doubt Luke took a great deal of trouble to get his facts right (Luke 1:1-4). He talked to those who had known Jesus personally. He worked and travelled with Paul on some occasions. That's when he writes 'we' did this or that (*one example:* Acts 15:11-40). On another of these occasions (Acts 21:8), Luke met up with Philip the evangelist in Caesarea. Many people believe that it was then that he also met up with Mary, the mother of Jesus in her old age and learned all that he records in the early chapters of his Gospel.

PLAN to read through the whole book of the *Acts of the Apostles*. We've already looked at some of it in our Bible readings, but if you can set aside an hour or two for a complete read in one sitting, you are in for an exciting experience.

NOTICE that every now and then, Luke, the author, puts in a summary verse about how the good news about Jesus is spreading. Check out Acts 6:7; 8:4; 9:31; 12:24; 16:5; 28:31.

extra

New horizons

WHAT NEXT!

You've finished this book. What are you going to do about Bible reading now? Well, for a start, there are four other *Growing with Jesus* books. If you have already worked through all of those, Scripture Union offers a choice of three different styles of notes for adults. One of them should suit you!

You may order GWJ books and Scripture Union notes from
- your local Christian bookshop • your Scripture Union church representative
- by post from Scripture Union Mail order.

SU ADULT BIBLE READING NOTES

DAILY BREAD Practical help from the Bible for everyday Christian living. £1.60 quarterly

ALIVE TO GOD Bible exploration for living by the Spirit. £1.60 quarterly

DAILY NOTES An in-depth reflection for more experienced Bible readers. £1.60 quarterly

GROWING WITH JESUS SERIES

the ME problem by Rob Warner

the LOVE story by Lynn Green

the POWER dimension by Michael Cole

the GOD slot by Philip Mohabir

the PRAYER principle by Jim Graham

ORDER FORM

To: Scripture Union Mail Order, 9-11 Clothier Road, Bristol BS4 5RL
Tel: (0272) 719709 24 hr order line Fax: (0272) 711672

GWJ Books	Total		Quantity	Price
Me problem (£2.25*)	_____	Daily Bread (£9.20*)	_____	_____
Love Story (£2.25*)	_____	Daily Notes (£9.20*)	_____	_____
Power dimension (£2.25*)	_____	Alive to God (£9.20*)	_____	_____
God slot (£2.25*)	_____	**Total**		
Prayer principle (£2.25*)	_____			

*Including UK postage and packing. (*Payment with order please*)

Please send me one year's supply of the above notes starting

☐ **January** ☐ **April** ☐ **July** ☐ **October** (*please tick one*)

Overseas rates Europe +£1.50 per subscription. Outside Europe +£3.00 per subscription.
PLEASE USE BLOCK CAPITALS

Name _____

Address _____

_____ Postcode _____

I enclose CHEQUE/POSTAL ORDER amount £ _____

Please debit my ACCESS/BARCLAYCARD amount £ _____

☐☐☐☐ ☐☐☐☐ ☐☐☐☐ ☐☐☐☐ Expiry date ☐☐☐☐

In **Australia**, write for subscription details to: Scripture Union, 241 Flinders Lane, Melbourne, Vic 3000.
In **USA**, write for subscription details to: Scripture Union, 7000 Ludlow Street, Upper Darby, PA 19082.
In **Canada**, write for subscription details to: Scripture Union, 1885 Clements Road, Unit 226, Pickering, Ontario, L1W 3V4. In **South Africa**, write for subscription details to: Scripture Union, Millard House, 83 Camp Ground Road, Rondebosch 7700.